SCIENCE QUEST

The Search for
Life in Space

by Clint Twist

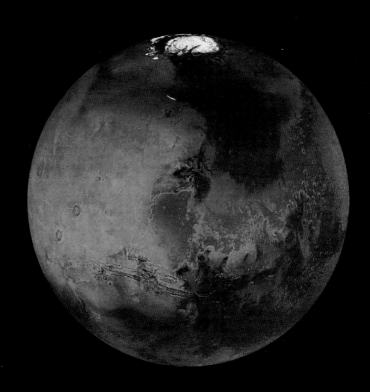

GARETH**STEVENS**
GS
PUBLISHING
A WRC Media Company

Please visit our web site at: www.garethstevens.com
For a free color catalog describing Gareth Stevens Publishing's list of high-quality books
and multimedia programs, call 1-800-542-2595 (USA) or 1-800-387-3178 (Canada).
Gareth Stevens Publishing's fax: (414) 332-3567.

Library of Congress Cataloging-in-Publication Data

Twist, Clint.
    The search for life in space / Clint Twist.— North American ed.
      p. cm. — (Science quest)
    Includes bibliographical references and index.
    ISBN 0-8368-4557-9 (lib. bdg.)
    1. Life on other planets—Juvenile literature. 2. Martians—Juvenile literature.
  3. Solar system—Juvenile literature. I. Title. II. Series.
    QB54.T95 2005
    576.8'39—dc22   2004059001

This North American edition first published in 2005 by
Gareth Stevens Publishing
A WRC Media Company
330 West Olive Street, Suite 100
Milwaukee, WI 53212 USA

This U.S. edition copyright © 2005 by Gareth Stevens, Inc. Original edition copyright © 2004 by ticktock Entertainment Ltd.
First published in Great Britain in 2004 by ticktock Media Ltd., Unit 2, Orchard Business Centre, North Farm Road, Tunbridge
Wells, Kent, TN2 3XF.

Gareth Stevens editor: Carol Ryback
Gareth Stevens designer: Kami M. Koenig

Photo Credits: (t=top, b=bottom, c=center, l=left, r=right)
Alamy: 8(b), 10(tl). CORBIS: 10–11(c), 14(tl), 15 all, 20(bl), 24–25(c), 26(b). Hubble/NASA/ESA/ASU/J. Hester, P. Scowen: 7.
NASA: 5(tr), 6, 8(tr), 11(tr), 12(br), 12(l), 20(c), 24(l). NASA/JPL/Cornell: 12(c). Naval Research Laboratory: 9. Rex Features:
21(r), 29(br). Science Photo Library: 2–3, 4–5(c), 12(cr), 13(t), 16, 17, 18(tl), 18–19(c), 19(r), 21(br), 22(c), 23 all, 27 all,
28, 29(t).

Printed in the United States of America

1 2 3 4 5 6 7 8 9 09 08 07 06 05

Contents

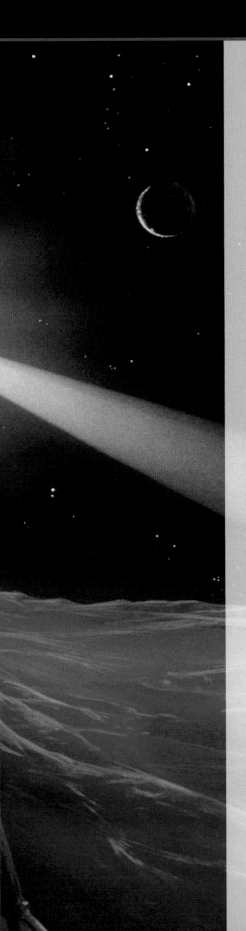

Words that appear in the glossary are printed in
boldface type the first time they occur in the text.

Introduction

Peple have been studying night skies and the **stars** for thousands of years. Ancient **astronomers** in different lands gave different names to the brightest stars in the sky. They also gave names to the **constellations** — the patterns that some stars appear to form in the sky. The Greeks knew that most stars remain in the same fixed pattern but that some "stars" also appeared to travel across the sky. They named these wandering objects **planets**. For centuries, people believed the ancient Greek idea that Earth was the center of the **universe**, and that the **Sun**, the stars, and the planets followed an **orbit** around Earth.

The Earth in Space

The invention of the telescope in the early seventeenth century provided astronomers with an improved view of the universe and helped them develop a better understanding of how it operated. After much controversy, they finally accepted the idea that Earth and the other planets orbit the Sun, and that stars are in fact very distant suns. As the science and technology of **astronomy** progressed, further discoveries revealed distant galaxies and even determined the life cycles of stars. During the twentieth century, astronomy took a giant leap forward with the introduction of radio telescopes, artificial **satellites**, and manned spaceflight. Astronomers and **astrophysicists** used their new tools to study images of strange and fascinating objects, such as **supernovae**, **nebulae**, and **pulsars**.

The Mauna Kea Observatory in Hawaii constantly scans the stars and planets of our solar system and beyond.

▲ *The* Hubble Space Telescope (HST) *allows astronomers to see far beyond our solar system.*

Extraterrestrials?

As scientists learned more about the universe, they began to wonder about the possibilities of **extraterrestrial** life — life-forms on other planets. Percival Lowell, a nineteenth-century astronomer, truly believed he had discovered a sure sign of extraterrestrial life when he announced the presence of "canals" on the surface of Mars. He turned out to be mistaken, and some scientists predicted that we would never find life beyond Earth. So far, these predictions have proved true. For instance, when astronauts landed on the **Moon** in 1969, they found no signs of life. Robot spacecraft since then found no evidence of life on Venus, Mars, or any other planets. But this lack of evidence does not mean that extraterrestrial life does not exist. It just means that we have not found it yet. We must keep searching.

Alone In Space?

Astronomers expect the unexpected when studying the universe, and they have discovered many strange and wonderful things. They have photographed the birth of new stars and detected the strange objects created when old stars explode and die. So far, astronomers have found no signs of intelligent life elsewhere in our **solar system** or the universe. Still, some people remain convinced it is only a matter of time before we catch sight of alien spaceships speeding toward Earth.

Alien Invasion

At the end of the nineteenth century, science fiction author H. G. Wells wrote *War of the Worlds*, in which Martians armed with futuristic war machines and death rays invaded Earth. In 1938, in honor of the fortieth anniversary of the novel, actor Orson Welles aired a dramatized version of the book on the radio. (Television was not invented yet, so people gathered around their radios for entertainment.) Despite warnings that it was a fictional account, the broadcast sounded so much like a news report that thousands of people believed Martians had actually invaded Earth. Widespread panic resulted.

Searching Our Solar System

Today, scientists believe it is very unlikely that beings from another planet will ever invade Earth. None of the other planets in our solar system shows any signs of life. If scientists do eventually discover life on other solar system planets, it will most likely be in a simple form, such as **bacteria**, rather than advanced, intellectual aliens. The more scientists learn about the universe, however, the more they realize how little they actually know for certain. Ten years ago, the idea of **extrasolar** planets (planets beyond our solar system) was just a theory. Since then, astronomers have indirectly located more than 120 extrasolar planets.

SCIENCE CONCEPTS

The Speed of Light

A light-year measures distance, not time. Light travels 186,000 miles per second (300,000 kilometers per second). Scientists measure the enormous distances between objects in the universe using the speed of light. One light-year equals 6 trillion miles (10 trillion km), the distance light travels in one year.

▲ *A stunning image taken by the HST shows an array of distant galaxies many light-years from Earth.*

This **false-color** image of the "Pillars of Creation" in *the* Eagle Nebula *is probably the most famous image taken by the* Hubble Space Telescope. *A nebula is akin to a star nursery where stars are "born" from clouds of dust and gases. Astronomers believe that the pillar on the left measures about four light-years (see "Science Concepts," page 6) from top to bottom.* The Eagle Nebula *is located roughly 6,500 light-years from Earth. This portion of it would look like dull gray clouds through your telescope.*

Limited View

Telescopes become more powerful each year, but even the best provide astronomers with only brief glimpses of events in the universe. While the billions and billions of stars are the most numerous objects in the universe, stars like our Sun, with numerous planets circling it, are rare. Some stars are much younger than the Sun, and many are just forming inside dust clouds far out in space. Other stars are much older than the Sun. A star near the end of its life span may blow apart in a gigantic supernova explosion that leaves behind a **neutron star**. Some stars inflate slowly and change color, while other stars appear to shrink and fade away. Planets capable of supporting life may orbit a number of these stars. The question remains: Which stars have planets?

SCIENCE SNAPSHOT

Scientists use images taken by the HST to create beautiful "false-color" images of nebulae, **galaxies**, and other **celestial bodies**. After they delete the "junk" streaks, they use four filters that see the light produced by specific atoms in the objects. The blue, green, and red filters screen for **oxygen**, **hydrogen**, and sulfur atoms, respectively. When combined with the fourth filter (a starlight filter) a breathtaking final image results.

Spacey Neighborhood

The nearest star to Earth is the Sun. As stars go, ours is fairly typical. It's not the biggest, nor the brightest, nor the youngest, nor the oldest. What makes our star special among the billions of stars in the universe is the fact that nine planets orbit around it, and one of them — Earth — supports life. Our star and its planets form what is known as the solar system.

Our Location

We live in the **Milky Way Galaxy**. A galaxy consists of billions of stars held together by the force of **gravity**. Most galaxies also contain enormous clouds of dust and gas. The Milky Way is shaped like a huge convex lens — fatter in the middle than at the edges. The entire galaxy rotates, which produces several spiral arms that extend from its center. Our solar system is located in one of those spiral arms. The Milky Way Galaxy measures about 100,000 light-years in diameter. The nearest similar galaxy is the Andromeda Galaxy, about two million light-years away.

*The Sun, the planets, the asteroid belt between Mars and Jupiter, and a **comet**.*

SCIENCE CONCEPTS

Gravity Rules

Gravity is the strongest force in the universe and the only force that operates over immense distances. Gravity is a property of mass — the more mass an object has, the stronger its gravity. We experience gravity as a one-way attracting force between objects. Earth's gravity holds objects on its surface instead of letting them fly off into space. The Sun has millions of times more mass than the Earth, so its gravity is strong enough to hold the planets together in their orbits over distances of hundreds of millions of miles (km). Gravity from the planets also affects the Sun's orbit, but only very slightly.

Orbiting around a Star

The Sun's gravity holds the planets in place as if they were attached to it by invisible strings. Earth, the third planet, orbits the Sun at a distance of about 93 million miles (150 million km). Only Mercury and Venus are closer. Earth takes one year to complete an orbit around its star. Jupiter orbits the Sun at a distance of about 485 million miles (780 million km), and one orbit lasts nearly twelve Earth years.

SCIENCE SNAPSHOT

Astronomers use the **Astronomical Unit (A.U.)** to measure the distance between Earth and the Sun: 1 A.U. is the same as 93 million miles (150 million km). They measure the extreme distances between our solar system and other stars or galaxies using light-years. For instance, the next nearest star to Earth, Alpha Centauri C, is 4.25 light-years away.

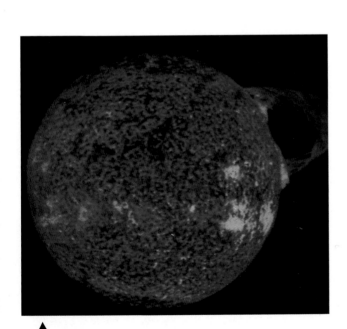

Our Sun is an exploding ball of gas 300,000 times the size of Earth. The Sun's nuclear energy makes life on Earth possible.

A Range of Planets

Our solar system has two basic types of planets: small, rocky planets and large, gaseous planets. Mercury, Venus, Earth, and Mars are rocky planets. Jupiter, Saturn, Uranus, and Neptune are gas planets. Astronomers believe that Pluto is formed from a mixture of rocks and ice. Most of the planets have one or more moons (natural satellites). Jupiter, with a diameter of about 88,860 miles (143,000 km), is one-tenth the size of the Sun and by far the largest of the planets. Jupiter also contains more than twice as much mass as all the other nine planets put together.

Water covers about 70 percent of our planet's surface and is essential to life on Earth.

Earth is a very comfortable place to live. Scientists have identified more than one million different plant and animal species. They believe Earth has millions more species that await discovery. As far as we know, Earth is the only place in the universe where life exists. What makes Earth so special?

Water

Earth looks blue from space because water covers two-thirds of its surface. Near the poles, water is frozen into ice, but most of Earth's water is in liquid form in freshwater lakes and the salty oceans. The bodies of most living things (including humans) are composed mainly of water. Water is liquid only at temperatures between 32° Fahrenheit (0° Celsius) and 212° F (100° C). Most species survive within a much narrower range of temperatures. One of the main reasons for life on Earth is that the planet receives just the right amount of energy from its star to produce mild surface temperatures. Astronomers believe that other planets within our solar system or beyond that show signs of having water might also support life.

SCIENCE CONCEPTS

Vital Elements

Most life on Earth, from the simple one-celled plants and animals, to the incredibly complicated human body, is based on **carbon**. Researchers have also found sulfur-based organisms living in extreme conditions, such as near the boiling **hydrothermal vents** deep on the Pacific Ocean floor. Scientists searching for life elsewhere in the universe realize that it could be based on any chemical, but they believe that looking for carbon life-forms affords the best chances of success.

Air

Earth's **atmosphere** forms an airy blanket around the planet. It contains a mixture of gases, including water vapor, nitrogen, oxygen, and carbon dioxide. The atmosphere also keeps Earth's temperatures mild and allows water to circulate as different forms of precipitation. The many layers of the atmosphere help shield Earth from some of the Sun's harmful energy, especially **ultraviolet** (**UV**) rays.

Earth's oceans, atmosphere, and magnetic field work together to support life.

Magnetism

Planet Earth has a molten iron core. As Earth rotates, it spins and sloshes its liquid core around deep inside the Earth. The circulation of this liquid metal creates a strong magnetic field that reaches out into space around the planet. The magnetic field deflects much of the Sun's harmful energy away from Earth. It also traps charged particles, such as protons and electrons, to form the **Van Allen radiation belts**.

A lizard is a notable example of the variety of life on Earth.

SCIENCE SNAPSHOT

Earth orbits the Sun inside what some scientists like to call the "**Goldilocks Zone**" — the "just right" region of space around a star that creates conditions capable of supporting carbon-based life. Our solar system's Goldilocks Zone is narrow. Mercury and Venus are too close to the Sun and too hot for life. Mars is almost (but not quite) right for life as we know it. The other planets are much too cold and far from the Sun to harbor life.

M ars, often called the Red Planet, is Earth's most similar neighbor. The fourth planet, it orbits the Sun at a distance of about 142 million miles (228 million km), near the outer edge of the Goldilocks Zone. People have long wondered about the possibility of life on Mars. None of the scientific expeditions revealed evidence of life on Mars.

Dry and Cold

Bare rock, stones, and red iron oxide (rusty) dust make up the surface of Mars. Its thin atmosphere is composed mostly of carbon dioxide gas. A light coating of frozen carbon dioxide ("dry ice") crowns the north and south poles. Daytime temperatures can reach higher than 100° F (38° C) and fall below -200° F (-128°C) at night. Dangerous UV rays bombard Mars's surface and enormous dust storms swirl around the planet. Mars shows no sign of carbon-based life. Long ago, however, life on Mars may have thrived.

The Mars Spirit *rover captured an image of the circular "Sleepy Hollow" feature about five days after it landed in early 2004.*

Searching For Life

Spacecraft have examined much of Mars's surface with powerful cameras. Robot landers sampled Mars's dirt and rocks. None of the tests revealed evidence of animal or plant life. The landers also conducted chemical tests that checked for microscopic life, such as bacteria. All these tests proved negative — so far, Mars shows no signs of life. Tests performed by the *Opportunity* rover in 2004 determined that water once flowed over the planet's red surface, forming gullies and shaping the vast plains.

SCIENCE CONCEPTS

Earth

Mars

Lost Atmosphere

Millions of years ago, Mars probably had an atmosphere similar to that found on Earth. At about half the size of Earth, Mars has much less mass, and therefore, weak gravity — so weak, in fact, that it cannot hold onto its own atmosphere. Most of Mars's atmosphere gradually drifted into space. Also, because Mars does not have a molten iron core, it lacks a magnetic field. Nothing protects the Red Planet from the damaging effects of the **electromagnetic spectrum**.

A Once-Watery World

On Earth, the presence of water often indicates the presence of life. If water once existed on Mars, maybe it also once harbored life. Some scientists believe that billions of years ago, oceans, rivers, and a thicker atmosphere covered Mars. They point to surface features, such as gullies and valleys, that look as if running water formed them. Scientists have also identified areas that resemble dried-up riverbeds. Thorough examinations of martian rocks by the landers confirmed that some formed in the presence of water. No water or life currently exists on the Red Planet. Mars's small size and weak gravity worked against any long-term survival for life-forms, and the fourth planet lost its precious atmosphere and other resources to space.

SCIENCE SNAPSHOT

Sometimes **meteorites** that hit Mars chip off tiny chunks of the Red Planet's surface. Once kicked into space, these chunks become meteorites that may impact Earth's surface. Scientists often use electron microscopes to analyze meteorites. Some claim that these tests revealed structures resembling the remains of living cells. Other scientists, however, are not convinced that these cell-like structures are proof of life on Mars.

Historical map of the surface of Mars by the Italian astronomer Giovanni Schiaparelli (1835–1910).

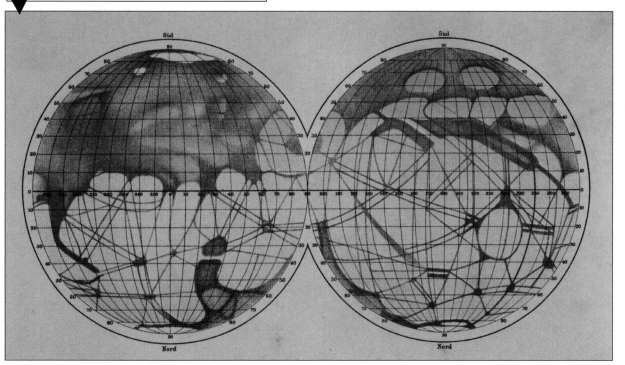

An array of radio telescopes beneath a large, false-color image of the Whirlpool Galaxy.

R adio signals, or waves, travel to Earth from distant stars and galaxies. Every radio wave scientists have detected so far is simply radio "noise" produced by a variety of natural sources. Some astronomers believe that among all this noise from space, they might just find some radio waves produced by other forms of intelligent life. Radio astronomers use large metal dishes (known as radio telescopes) to detect radio waves from space.

Radio Astronomy

Radio telescopes detect radio signals from space. Objects that appear faint through a light telescope may appear very "bright" through a radio telescope. Vibrating gas molecules in space produce the weakest radio waves. Shock waves and magnetic fields created by supernovae and **black holes** generate the most powerful radio signals. So far, astronomers have detected only natural forms of radio signals from outer space.

SETI

In the 1960s, radio astronomers began searching for signs of life elsewhere in the universe. Their project became known as the **Search for Extraterrestrial Intelligence** (**SETI**). First, scientists had to decide exactly what they were searching for; second, they had to know where to look. They quickly realized that intelligent beings would repeat a radio message over and over again. Deciding where to look proved much more difficult.

SCIENCE CONCEPTS

Visible Spectrum

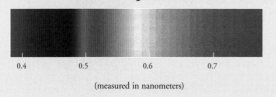

0.4   0.5   0.6   0.7

(measured in nanometers)

The Electromagnetic Spectrum

The light and colors that we see make up only a small part of the electromagnetic spectrum. Radio waves, ultraviolet waves, X-rays, and gamma rays are a few of the other parts of the electromagnetic spectrum. They each give off energy with a different wavelength. Most wavelengths are so tiny that the metric system is used to measure them. Visible light's wavelength is measured in nanometers — ten-millionths of a millimeter. The wavelengths of X-rays and gamma rays are up to one million times shorter than those of visible light. Gravity is not part of the electromagnetic spectrum.

Pulsars

A pulsar is a rapidly rotating, **super-dense** neutron star that sends out two beams of radio energy from each of its magnetic poles. When such beams, or pulses, "flash" Earth, they appear as regularly timed, auditory lighthouse beams from space. In 1967, British astrophysicist Jocelyn Bell Burnell discovered the first pulsar. It pulses every 1.3 seconds. Since then, scientists have identified hundred of pulsars with pulse rates that vary from a fraction of a second to four seconds.

Frank Drake, Chairman of the Board of Trustees for SETI, and Jill Cornell Tarter, director of the Center for SETI Research, hope to someday detect radio signals produced by intelligent beings.

Professor Carlos Calle, of Sweet Briar College in Sweet Briar, Virginia, adjusts interferometry instruments.

Planets that orbit stars beyond our solar system are simply too small to see through telescopes. Astronomers must identify these extrasolar planets using special techniques. They set up telescopes to watch for stars that appear to "wobble," or vary slightly from their normal orbit. A planet orbiting near a star can cause such wobbling.

How Gravity Causes Wobbling

While our massive star produces a gravitational force strong enough to hold the solar system's planets in their orbits, gravity from the planets, especially the two largest, Jupiter and Saturn, affects our Sun's orbit as well. If we could view our solar system from about ten light-years away, we would see a slight but regular wobble in the Sun's path through space. Wobble watching is the surest indication that a large object orbits a distant star. Two different techniques help astronomers detect such gravitational wobbles.

Interferometry

Astronomers start their search for a wobbling star by accurately measuring the "target" star's position every night for several months. If a star wobbles, its position will vary slightly during that time period. Astronomers obtain the most accurate measurements of a star's wobble using a special technique called **interferometry**. Two different telescopes, sometimes many miles (km) apart, act as one telescope to simultaneously measure that star's position. When combined, the two sets of measurements yield the exact amount of wobble.

SCIENCE CONCEPTS

Orbital Planes

Our solar system is basically flat, thanks to the delicate balance between the Sun's powerful gravity and the forces produced by each planet's high-speed motion through space. Eight planets orbit

the Sun in an almost perfectly circular orbit within the same flat plane of space. Only Pluto, the outermost planet, displays a different balance. Its strongly **elliptical** orbit lies at an angle to the other planetary orbits.

Doppler Color Shift

A wobbling star changes color slightly but on a regular basis as it moves back and forth in space. Interferometry helps astronomers measure the side-to-side wobble of a star. The **Doppler effect** helps them detect a star's back-and-forth wobble by analyzing the color of light it emits. Light from a star approaching our solar system displays "blueshift." It appears bluer than normal as the wavelength of its light shifts toward the shorter, "blue" end of the visible spectrum. Wavelengths of light from a star speeding away from our solar system become longer. They display "redshift" and give the object a redder than normal appearance. Astronomers search for light from a star that regularly shifts from red to blue. The shifting indicates that gravity from a nearby planet is probably causing the wobble.

Hawaii's "twin" Keck telescopes on Mauna Kea scan the universe.

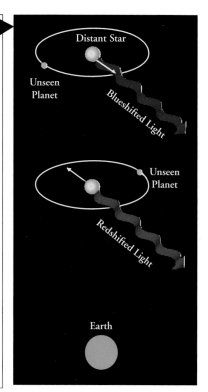

Gravity from an unseen planet acting on a distant star causes the star to shift in its orbit. The shifting changes the wavelength of the light emitted by the star, so an observer on Earth sees that star's light change color. As the star moves slightly closer to Earth, its light will blueshift; slightly farther and the light redshifts.

Distant Star

Unseen Planet

Blueshifted Light

Unseen Planet

Redshifted Light

Earth

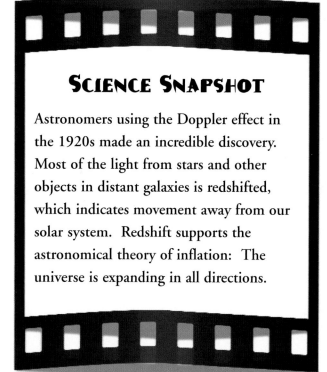

SCIENCE SNAPSHOT

Astronomers using the Doppler effect in the 1920s made an incredible discovery. Most of the light from stars and other objects in distant galaxies is redshifted, which indicates movement away from our solar system. Redshift supports the astronomical theory of inflation: The universe is expanding in all directions.

B y the end of the 1980s, several teams of astronomers concentrated on searching for signs of extrasolar planets. Although convinced that these planets existed, astronomers needed proof. When they did discover an extrasolar planet, it was not what they had expected.

Planets Around Pulsars

The astronomers who made the first extrasolar discovery of a planet were not looking for planets around nearby stars. Instead, they were using radio telescopes to study the faint pulsar in an area of space now known as the PSR B1257 + 12 planetary system, located more than 1,000 light-years from Earth. The pattern of radio signals from the pulsar was irregular. Radio astronomers realized that only an unseen large object, such as a planet, orbiting nearby could explain the irregularity. The gravity produced by such a planet (or planets) made the pulsar wobble very slightly, causing the irregular radio signals. Additional measurements confirmed the

A fictional view of a pulsar, seen from a nearby planet. A pulsar rotates rapidly, flashing radio signals — much like a celestial lighthouse.

presence of three small planets in PSR B1257+12. Each planet is about the size of Earth or Mars and takes between 25 and 99 days to orbit the pulsar. They have not been named and are known by the letters a, b, and c. Scientists do not believe that there is life on these pulsar planets. If they existed before the supernova that produced the pulsar, the planets will have been burned clean by the explosion. If they were formed during the supernova, life will not have had time to develop. Also, if the pulsar's radio beam sweeps across the planets, its energy at such a close distance would kill any living thing.

SCIENCE CONCEPTS

Familiar Patterns

We are now certain that the Sun is not the only star with planets, but we have not yet discovered any other systems of planets like our own solar system. Most of the extrasolar planets so far discovered follow the same pattern as *51 Pegasi B* — a single large planet orbiting very closely around a star. These planets are known as Pegasian planets, and they appear to be the most common type of planet in the universe.

Other Jupiters

In 1995, the patience of some dedicated wobble watchers was finally rewarded — they discovered a large planet orbiting around a nearby Sunlike star. Astronomers used the Doppler effect to study light from the star *51 Pegasi*, about 50 light-years from Earth. They detected alternating red-blue light shifts, indicating that a nearby planet may be causing the wobbling. The amount of wobble showed that it was indeed a large planet, exactly what they expected. The Jupiter-sized planet, known as *51 Pegasi B*, orbits eight times closer to its star than Mercury is to our Sun. That means *51 Pegasi B* orbits not in a Goldilocks Zone but in a "burned-to-a-crisp" zone: There is no possibility of life on *51 Pegasi B*.

An artist's impression of 47 Ursa Majoris B, *an extrasolar planet that some scientists believe may have water-bearing moons.*

Swiss astrophysicist Michel Mayor helped discover 51 Pegasi B *in 1995.*

SCIENCE SNAPSHOT

One star may have an entire system of planets. Astronomers have detected a Jupiter-sized planet orbiting around the star *47 Ursa Majoris*. This planet (called *47 Ursa Majoris B*) differs from Pegasian planets because it orbits the star at about the same distance as Mars is from the Sun. Although it has not yet been confirmed, *47 Ursa Majoris* may well have one or more Earth-sized planets within its Goldilocks Zone.

Making Contact

Some scientists argue that other forms of intelligent life must exist somewhere among the billions of stars in the universe. Given that huge number of stars, the odds favor the chance that Earth is not unique in its ability to harbor life. Also, odds are that some of those other forms of life will be a lot more intelligent than we are, so we must look for advanced intelligences with very advanced technology.

Fruitless search?

Astronomers using the latest technologies have searched the universe for signs of intelligent life for nearly fifty years. So far they have found nothing whatsoever to suggest the presence of other intelligent beings in space. We also may not be capable of recognizing any signal they may have sent our way. Or, these beings with advanced intelligence may use their technology in ways that we can only imagine. For instance, they might have the technology that allows them to hide their planet from our view. The best explanation, however, is that any other intelligent life in the universe is simply too far away to contact us.

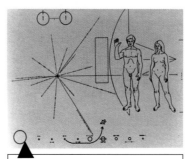

Just in case: Pioneer 10 *and* Pioneer 11 *each carry this plaque. It indicates their Earthly origin in hopes that an intelligent species sees it.*

Speeding to the Stars

Many astronomers believe that there is no point in making contact if visiting that faraway object is impossible. To understand why many scientists feel this way, we must consider how we measure speed on Earth. Since 1946, we have measured the speed of the fastest machines created so far using Mach numbers. "Mach 1" means the object travels at the speed of sound — 760 miles per hour (1200 kilometers per hour). The fastest jets travel at about Mach 5. A spaceship traveling at Mach 100 would take nearly 40,000 years to reach the nearest star. Allowing for accelerating

SCIENCE CONCEPTS

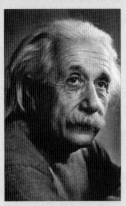

Great Ideas

Einstein's theories — the *Theory of Special Relativity* (1905) and the *Theory of General Relativity* (1916) — explain and predict the behavior of all large objects in the universe. The phrase "large objects" means anything larger than a single molecule. Other rules (known as quantum laws) govern what happens inside individual atoms and molecules. Many of the things predicted by Einstein's theories were not discovered until after his death. He predicted, for example, that powerful sources of gravity could "bend" light. Astronomers did not discover these **gravitational lenses** until the 1980s.

from a standstill and deceleration at the other end, a round-trip would take more than 100,000 years. Traveling at a faster speed would shorten the journey time. If we traveled at Mach 1,000,000, the round-trip would only take ten years, but we would run into a very serious problem on the way.

Fundamental Barrier

The problem is that Mach 1,000,000 is faster than the speed of light. According to the theories of Albert Einstein (1879–1955), it is impossible for anything to travel faster than light. Einstein demonstrated mathematically that a set of very strict rules govern the relationship of space, time, mass, and energy. Objects that increase their energy by traveling faster also increase their mass. At low speeds (below about Mach 1,000) the increase in mass is too small to have any effect. At faster speeds, an object's mass increases significantly, and the faster it travels, the greater the increase in its mass. According to Einstein's famous equation ($E=mc^2$), any object traveling at the speed of light would become too massive to move at all. Therefore, nothing can possibly travel faster than light.

Some people claim to have been abducted by aliens, and they often claim these alien beings resemble the one pictured here.

SCIENCE SNAPSHOT

There is a widespread belief that Earth is often visited by unidentified flying objects (UFOs). Pilots first reported sightings during World War II, and many other people claim to have seen UFOs. Despite all the claims, nobody has ever produced scientific evidence that UFOs exist.

Giant solar energy sails may propel future spacecraft at great speeds (but never faster than the speed of light) through space.

If scientists find signs of life on Mars, it will be one of the greatest discoveries of all time. It will change the way we think about life on Earth and about life elsewhere in the **universe**. Even if Mars has always been lifeless, however, it does not have to stay that way.

Shaping the Surface

If there is no martian life to preserve and study, it may be possible to **terraform** part of the Red Planet's surface. Terraforming is the process of changing the surface conditions on a planet so that it becomes more Earthlike. Mars is probably the most suitable planet in the solar system to terraform, but its weak gravity — not much more than one-third that of Earth's — presents a huge problem. The low gravity cannot hold an atmosphere on Mars's surface, and water cannot remain in a liquid state — it would immediately vaporize. Only an enclosed structure could contain an Earthlike atmosphere. Such an enclosure might even be large enough to contain an atmosphere that could create clouds and weather patterns. Centuries from now, we may develop the technology that increases Mars' gravity enough to hold an atmosphere with a surface pressure strong enough to keep water liquid. People could then live and breathe in the open.

Water and Air

Although there is currently no liquid water on Mars, data indicate that rocks just below the surface contain large amounts of frozen water—

A terraformed Mars would eventually allow us to live there without space suits.

maybe even enough to create lakes and oceans. We would need to develop a method for melting the frozen water and pumping it to the surface for use. Suggestions for melting the ice include using underground nuclear explosions. A less violent alternative is to place huge mirrors in orbit around Mars to direct sunlight onto specific areas of the Red Planet. During the summer season on Mars, when the carbon dioxide ice cap at the north pole disappears, such mirrors aimed at the north pole could raise temperatures and gradually melt the ice. Any liquid water produced would need to be immediately stored in a closed container. Another theoretically possible way to import water (in the form of ice) to Mars would be to collect it elsewhere — perhaps from the rings of Saturn. We could also invent solar-powered machines to break down some of that water into hydrogen and oxygen. The release of these gases into the contained atmosphere would help keep the air fresh.

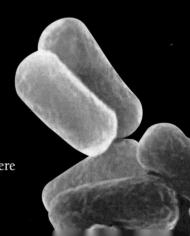

Creating an atmosphere on Mars might take hundreds of years. Meanwhile, explorers and colonists will have to wear space suits on the martian surface.

Life by Design

The twenty-first century science of genetic modification provides terraformers with some exciting new possibilities. Some bacteria can tolerate conditions almost as hostile as those found on the surface of Mars. Scientists may someday produce genetically modified bacteria that could survive on Mars. Bacteria that consume iron oxide and give off oxygen as a waste product would thrive on Mars because of its rusty, iron-oxide-covered surface. These bacteria would have plenty to eat, and would constantly release oxygen into the contained atmosphere.

We would need large amounts of oxygen-producing bacteria if we were to terraform Mars.

- Mars is just inside our solar system's Goldilocks Zone, which means it could potentially support life as we know it.
- Mars is the most similar planet to Earth and the most suitable for terraforming.
- There may be large quantities of water in the rocks beneath the martian surface.
- Mars is known as the Red Planet because its surface is stained red by iron oxide, or rust, deposits found there.
- Genetically modified bacteria could someday produce oxygen on Mars.
- Nuclear explosions set off deep below Mars's surface might release any water stored there, forming lakes or even oceans.

Case Study: Beneath Unearthly Seas

If Mars proves lifeless, we will not stop searching for life in our solar system. Life may not exist on any of the other planets, but we may discover it on one of the many moons that **orbit** the outer planets. Europa, one of Jupiter's numerous moons, is the most likely candidate.

Trail of Discovery

Galileo discovered Jupiter's four largest moons — Io, Europa, Ganymede, and Callisto — in 1610. These moons are visible from Earth with an ordinary telescope or even with binoculars! In the 1970s, *Voyager 1* and 2 spacecraft captured the first close look at these Galilean moons. The many exciting discoveries included finding an active volcano on the surface of Io and a smooth layer of ice covering Europa. Astronomers wondered if the interior of Europa was warm enough for liquid water to exist deep beneath the icy surface. In the 1990s, the *Galileo* spacecraft obtained higher quality photographs of Europa's surface. Some of the features shown in the new photographs suggest that liquid water lies much closer to the surface than previously suspected. Europa's ice is probably less than 0.6 miles (1 km) thick. Some astrophysicists believe that this thin, icy crust may protect an ocean of liquid water that may harbor life.

Giant tube worms live on bacteria that don't need sunlight or oxygen. Perhaps a similar food chain exists on Europa.

A spectacular view of the craggy surface of Jupiter's moon, Europa.

An artist's impression of a robot submarine burrowing through Europa's icy crust in search of life.

Warmth and Life?

Europa is too far from the Sun to receive much heat, so its ocean surface remains cold and frozen. Beneath the ice, however, things may be different. Europa's ocean is probably kept liquid thanks to heat from its interior, which is probably made of molten rock. Astronomers believe that Europa might have undersea volcanoes. If so, it would be an extremely exciting discovery: Undersea volcanoes and hydrothermal vents on Earth provide a habitat for some of the strangest forms of life found here. Deep beneath the Atlantic and Pacific oceans, hydrothermal vents and chimneys known as "black smokers" provide chemical food for bacteria and about three hundred other species that survive without sunlight or oxygen. Other strange creatures, such as giant tube worms, blind shrimp, and colorless crabs, feed on bacteria and other organisms living near these vents. Life on Europa is therefore possible, and further exploration is already planned.

Submarine through Space?

An *Explorer* spacecraft will be sent to orbit about 125 miles (200 km) above Europa's frozen surface. The Explorer will use a high-power **radar** system to map the extent of Europa's subsurface water. If the *Explorer* confirms the existence of large seas, the next stage will land a robot submarine on Europa. The submarine will melt its way through the ice and then sink down below the surface to search for signs of life.

Case Study: A New Planet in the Solar System

Space is full of surprises, and nobody can tell when or where the next discovery will occur. By the end of the twentieth century, most scientists were convinced that they had mapped and measured the entire solar system. The recent discovery of other "planets" beyond the orbit of Pluto has forced them to redraw their maps of nearby space.

The Discovery of Pluto

The outermost planet, Pluto, was discovered in 1930 by Clyde Tombaugh. He patiently studied faint objects in the sky, night after night. An object that appeared fixed in place was a star, but one that appeared to move slightly but steadily across the sky was a planet. Some astronomers argue that Pluto is not a true planet because it does not fit the pattern of the rest of the planets in the solar system. Pluto is very small and follows an elliptical orbit shaped like a squashed circle. It also orbits at a different angle to the Sun and the planets. Despite these differences, astronomers consider Pluto the ninth planet.

Stretching the Solar System

Astronomers using the powerful telescopes of the twenty-first century have already made some startling discoveries. By following Tombaugh's technique, they located other "planets" orbiting the Sun. The largest and most distant of these, Sedna, was discovered in 2003. Sedna is about 994 miles (1,600 km) in diameter. It orbits the Sun at a distance of about 8 billion miles (13 billion km) — about three times farther away than Pluto. Sedna takes roughly 10,500 years to complete one orbit. Some scientists describe Sedna as a "planetoid," but others argue that if Pluto is a planet, then Sedna is also a planet. Future astronomers may reclassify Pluto as the nearest example of an altogether different type of object, rather than an actual planet like the others in the solar system.

Astronomer Clyde Tombaugh discovered Pluto in 1930.

The Outer Limits

Our solar system contains a lot more than major objects such as the Sun, the planets, and their moons. Thousands of **asteroids** — lumps of rock and metal varying from the size of a bus to about 622 miles (1,000 km) in diameter — orbit the Sun between Mars and Jupiter in a region called the asteroid belt. Some astronomers consider the largest asteroids minor planets. The **Oort Cloud**, a region of space filled with **comets**, marks the outermost limits (about one-half of a light-year from the Sun) of the solar system. A comet is a dirty snowball made of ice and dust. Comets are smaller than most asteroids and have much less mass.

Background: An artist's impression of Sedna.

Inset: Pluto and its moon, Charon.

According to Albert Einstein, we may never travel to the **stars** because the distances are too great and we cannot travel faster than the speed of light. One day, however, we may build spaceships that can carry human passengers between the galaxies. Some even believe that we will one day discover how to travel across the **universe** by way of black holes and **wormholes**.

Black Holes

A black hole forms when a very large star explodes. Any matter left behind collapses in upon itself, getting smaller even as its mass increases. The tightly compressed collapsed matter "disappears" from the universe and creates a black hole. The gravity of a black hole is so strong that it sucks in everything around it, including light. A black hole the size of a golf ball could absorb Earth without growing larger itself. A Jupiter-sized black hole would contain more mass than one billion stars. A glowing disk, called an **accretion disk**, surrounds an active black hole. An inactive black hole is simply that — a black hole, invisible against the blackness of space.

The enormous gravity of a black hole (orange) slowly pulls a giant star (blue) into its center.

Wormholes

An inactive black hole is invisible only in terms of visible light. If you could "see" with gravity, the picture would be very different. Black holes, even small ones, produce incredibly concentrated gravity much stronger than the gravity of stars and galaxies. Some astronomers believe that a black hole's gravity is strong enough to bore a hole through space to another dimension of **space-time**. These holes are named wormholes, although nobody knows for sure whether or not they exist. If wormholes do exist, they could provide future explorers with a way of traveling through the universe. Wormholes may turn out to be short-cuts to the stars, or they could take us even further.

Destination: Unknown

A wormhole might, for example, lead to another part of our universe that is hundreds of light-years from Earth. In that case, the explorers would know where they were, but we would never know what happened to them. According to some theories, wormholes might be gateways to different universes. Explorers sent through these wormholes would have no idea where they were. Another theory says that a wormhole could lead to the same place in the same universe, but at a different time — which would make a wormhole function like a time machine. Whatever the destination, no one can guarantee that human passengers would survive a journey through a wormhole. The force of gravity might be strong enough to pull their bodies apart in a process known as **spaghettification**.

Glossary

accretion disk: materials that form in the shape of a rotating disk around an object in space.

asteroids: random rocks speeding through space and ranging in size from the size of a bus to 600 miles (1,000 km) in diameter.

astronomers: scientists who study stars and space.

Astronomical Unit (A.U.): a unit that represents the distance between Earth and the Sun. It is used to compare distances, such as between planets in our solar system and the Sun as well as their distance from Earth.

astronomy: the study of the stars and space.

astrophysicists: scientists who study the life cycles of and relationships between stars, planets, and other objects in the universe.

atmosphere: a layer of gas held near the surface of a planet or moon by its gravity.

bacteria: group of single-celled organisms that are among the simplest forms of known life.

black holes: objects with immensely strong gravity — strong enough to "suck in" light. Black holes form when a supergiant star collapses.

carbon: one of the chemical elements that is an essential part of all "living" chemistry.

celestial: related to the sky, stars, and planets.

comets: masses of ice and dust up to 31 miles (50 km) in diameter that orbit the Sun. A comet travels throughout the solar system and returns to Earth's view at predictable times.

constellations: the patterns formed by apparent groupings of stars.

Doppler effect: variations in light, radio, or sound waves that can change in frequency according to whether an object is moving toward or away from an observer.

electromagnetic spectrum: the various wavelengths of energy, such as radio waves, infrared waves, visible light, ultraviolet, X-rays, and gamma rays, that travel through space.

elliptical: oval-shaped.

extrasolar: anything beyond our solar system.

extraterrestrial: anything that originates somewhere other than Earth.

false-color: a technique that adds unnatural colors to images of celestial objects.

galaxies: collections of billions of stars held together in space by gravity.

gravitational lenses: situations in space, caused by gravity's effect on the electromagnetic spectrum, that produce an image (visual or otherwise) of a star or planet not normally detected.

gravity: a property of mass and density that produces an unopposed attracting force. Gravity is the strongest force in the universe.

Goldilocks Zone: the region around a star in which conditions are suitable for life as we know it to exist.

hydrogen: the simplest and most abundant chemical element in the universe. Hydrogen is the basic fuel of stars; it also combines with oxygen to make water.

hydrothermal vents: cracks in the Earth's crust deep on the ocean floor from which boiling water flows. Many strange creatures live around these vents.

interferometry: a technique that uses at least two telescopes some distance apart to simultaneously measure the position of an object in space.

light-year: the distance traveled by light in one year and the basic unit for measuring the universe.

meteorites: chunks of matter that break off planets and travel through space to impact other planets or moons in the solar system.

Milky Way Galaxy: the galaxy in which our solar system is located.

Moon: Earth's natural satellite; also, an object with a fixed orbit around a planet.

nebulae: star-forming regions in space.

neutron star: an object made of super-dense matter produced by a supernova. Rapidly rotating neutron stars are called pulsars.

Oort Cloud: a region at the outermost reaches of our solar system that contains millions of comets.

orbit : the usually somewhat circular path through space made by an object that is held in place by the gravity of a more massive object at its center.

oxygen: a chemical element that exists in Earth's atmosphere as a gas. Oxygen is essential to nearly all forms of life on Earth.

planets: large objects, composed of rock, gas, or a combination of both, that orbit a star.

pulsars: rapidly rotating neutron stars that emit beams of high-energy radio waves.

radar: an acronym for "**RA**dio **D**etecting **A**nd **R**anging," a technique that "bounces" radio signals off distant objects to determine information such as size, shape, and distance.

satellites: natural or artificial objects that orbit a larger body.

SETI: the **S**earch for **E**xtra**t**errestrial **I**ntelligence, a project that listens to and analyzes radio waves from space for signs of artificially created signals.

solar system: a Sun and the objects orbiting around it.

space-time: Einstein's theory that space and time are two ways of looking at the same thing, and that space-time forms the basic fabric of the universe.

spaghettification: the stretching of an object (until it looks like spaghetti noodles) by extreme forces of gravity.

stars: enormous, spinning masses of tightly compressed gases in space with their own power source and which emit many forms of radiation.

Sun: the star at the center of our solar system.

super-dense: matter that has been compressed by gravity into a much smaller volume than is normal for that amount of matter.

supernovae: massive explosions, caused by the collapse of giant stars, that radiate extreme amounts of electromagnetic radiation throughout the universe.

terraform: to alter surface conditions on a planet so that it resembles Earth and can support life.

ultraviolet (UV) rays: a type of electromagnetic radiation with shorter wavelengths than visible light; UV rays can damage living tissues.

universe: the entire field of outer space.

Van Allen radiation belts: areas of intense radiation trapped around Earth by its magnetic field.

wormholes: theoretical short-cuts through the universe that form when black holes bore through the fabric of space-time.

Index

accretion disks 28
aliens (*see* extraterrestrials)
Andromeda Galaxy 8
asteroids 8, 27
astronomers 4, 5, 6, 7, 10, 14, 15, 16, 17, 18, 19, 20, 24, 25, 26, 28
Astronomical Units (A.U.) 9
astronomy 4
astrophysicists 4, 19, 24
atmospheres 11, 12, 13, 22, 23

bacteria 6, 12, 23, 25
black holes 14, 28, 29
blueshift 17, 19
Burnell, Jocelyn Bell 15

carbon 10, 11, 12
carbon dioxide 11, 12, 22
comets 8, 27

Doppler effect 17, 19
Drake, Frank 15

Eagle Nebula 7
Earth 4, 5, 6, 7, 8, 9, 10, 11, 12, 13, 14, 15, 18, 20, 21, 22, 23, 25
Einstein, Albert 20, 21, 28
electromagnetic spectrum 14, 15
Europa 24, 25
extrasolar planets 6, 16, 18, 19
extraterrestrials 5, 6, 21

false-color images 7, 14

galaxies 6, 8, 9, 14, 17, 28
Galileo 24
genetic modification 23
Goldilocks Zone 11, 12, 19, 23
gravitational lenses 20
gravity 8, 9, 12, 13, 14, 15, 16, 17, 18, 20, 22, 28, 29

Hubble Space Telescope (HST) 5, 6, 7
hydrogen 7, 15, 22
hydrothermal vents 10, 25

ice 10, 22, 24, 25, 27
interferometry 16, 17

Jupiter 8, 9, 16, 19, 24, 25, 27
   moons of 24, 25

life-forms 5, 6, 10, 11, 12, 13, 18, 22, 24, 25, 28, 29
light-years 6, 7, 8, 9, 16, 18, 19, 27, 29
Lowell, Percival 5

magnetic fields 9, 12, 14
Mars 5, 8, 9, 11, 12, 13, 18, 19, 22, 23, 24, 27
Mauna Kea, Hawaii 4, 17
Mayor, Michel 19
Mercury 9, 11, 19
meteorites 13
moons 5, 9, 19, 24, 25

nebulae 4, 7
Neptune 9
neutron stars 7, 15, 29
nitrogen 11

Oort clouds 27
orbits 4, 9, 16, 18, 22, 26
oxygen 7, 11, 22, 23, 24

Pacific Ocean 10
planets 4, 6, 7, 8, 9, 10, 16, 17, 18, 19, 22, 24, 26, 27
Pluto 9, 16, 26, 27
pulsars 4, 15, 18

radar 25
radio telescopes 4, 14, 18
redshift 17, 19

satellites 4, 9
Saturn 9, 16, 22
Schiaparelli, Giovanni 13
Sedna 26, 27
SETI 14, 15
solar systems 6, 8, 9, 10, 16, 17, 18, 22, 24, 26, 27
spacecraft 5, 6, 12, 20, 24, 25, 28
space-time 28, 29
spaghettification 29
stars 4, 6, 7, 8, 9, 14, 15, 16, 17, 18, 19, 20, 26, 28
sulfur 7, 10
Suns 4, 7, 8, 9, 11, 12, 16, 18, 19, 25, 26, 27
supernovae 4, 7, 14, 18

Tarter, Jill Cornell 15
telescopes 4, 7, 14, 16, 24, 26
terraforming 22, 23
Tombaugh, Clyde 26

UFOs 21
ultraviolet light (UV) 11, 12
universe, the 4, 6, 7, 8, 10, 17, 18, 20, 22, 28, 29
Uranus 9

Van Allen radiation belts 11
Venus 5, 9, 11
volcanoes 24, 25

water 10, 11, 12, 13, 19, 22, 23, 24, 25
wormholes 28, 29